PATHS NOT PAVED

Collected Poems
by Lynne A. McNamara

Image on the cover:
Snowy Morning Sun,
Photo by Lynne A. McNamara

Image on frontispiece:
On a Walk in Rocky Mountain National Park,
Photo by Croi McNamara

Published by Buster Bodhi Press, LLC

All rights reserved. © 2025 Lynne A. McNamara
ISBN: 979-8-9991504-3-1
Library of Congress Control Number: 2025927568

Edited by Joseph Cavanaugh
Cover and book design by Mark Andrew James Terry
Photography by Lynne A. McNamara

Available on Amazon.com, Ingram Spark and most online book sellers

TABLE OF CONTENTS

7	Dedication	**45**	**Trusting Truths**
8	Photo: From NYC Over the Hudson	46	Side Dishes
9	Foreword	48	Peninsular
11	Introduction	49	Traveling to Topeka
		50	Where was I
13	**Yearning for More**	51	Boats of Burden
14	To Winter	52	Treasured
15	Questing	53	The Waitress
16	Not Quiet	54	Homecoming
17	My Muse	56	Photo: December Morning Moon in the West
18	Untethered		
19	On the Express Train	57	Lightning Bugs
20	Companions	58	Moon Moment
22	Eyes Yes	59	Love Isn't
23	If Only	60	I'm Always Here
24	Now Here		
25	Seeking Joy	**61**	**Paths Not Paved**
26	Breathing in the Breeze	62	Inside Insides
		63	The Rush
27	**Fleeting Mortality**	64	Sounding
28	One by One	65	Numbered No Ones
29	Death by Train	66	Medicine Wheel
30	Strangers	68	Photo: Eclipse Seen on the Sidewalk
31	Sakura Life		
32	Bald Eagle Bold	69	Deliverance
33	My Day	70	Stance
34	Continuous	72	Centering
35	High Flight	73	Jungle Lane
36	Bingo Queen and King	74	Body Beautiful
38	Photo: White Orchid	75	Camping
39	Her Song	76	The Child in Me
40	Ode to 2 Wheels	78	Photo: Rocky Mountain Stream
41	Gone	79	Voyage
42	The Old Bear	80	Sky Riding
44	Near Night	82	Photo: Country Acres Iris
		83	Where the Flowers Go
		84	Photo: Morning Setting Moon
		85	Acknowledgments
		86	Photo: White Mountain Shasta Daisy
		87	Lynne A. McNamara Biography
		88	Photo: Sunset Rays

I dedicate this book

to loved family and dear friends

who inspire me by who they are.

May awe-inviting clouds,

sunrises, sunsets, horizons,

mountains, and streams

move you and others

to take bountiful paths.

From NYC Over the Hudson

FOREWORD

In *Paths Not Paved*, Lynne McNamara doesn't ask for permission. The poems arrive quietly bare, unfiltered, and urgent. They slip beneath the surface of ordinary life, carrying with them the weight of unspoken emotions, unhealed memories, and the beauty found in even the most broken of places.

The poems in this collection are exactly that: quiet rebellions. They whisper against the noise of the world, revealing truths that many of us feel but struggle to name. They don't demand to be understood. Instead, they offer a mirror—to see ourselves more clearly, to feel more deeply, and to remember what it means to simply be.

Reading this book feels like being invited into something sacred. It's

> a chance to seek calm
> differences of maybes, perhaps
> adventures, out-of-the-way choices
>
> doorways, not better or worse
> but potent possibilities of courage
> to leave this path
>
> to explore, replenish this self
> the other within, who lacks time, energy—
> easy reasons to fear
>
> newness, other destinations.
> *(from "On the Express Train")*

Each poem is a fragment of a larger journey—one shaped by vulnerability, resilience, love, loss, and the unrelenting search for meaning. Some pieces strike like lightning. Others gently unfold, lingering in your thoughts long after the page is turned.

What makes this collection so special is its honesty. Lynne McNamara doesn't shy away from the raw or the tender. Her voice is clear, courageous, and deeply human. These poems don't pretend to hold all the answers, but they make the reader ask the right questions. And in that asking, they offer comfort to those who've felt alone in their wondering.

This is not just a book of poems. It's a conversation. Between Lynne and the page, between the words and the reader, between the silent spaces in us that long to be heard. Whether you move through these pages in order or find yourself returning to a single line again and again, I believe you'll discover something real in these pages: something that lingers, something that heals. I invite you to read this however you need to—from start to finish, or by letting your intuition flip to a random page. Either way, I hope you find something that lingers. A line that stays. A feeling that heals. A moment that reminds you: you are not alone.

Each piece feels like an open door into a private moment—sometimes tender, sometimes fierce, always true. There is a rhythm here that invites you to slow down and listen, to breathe, to reflect. Whether you're seeking solace, inspiration, or simply the comfort of knowing someone else has felt what you've felt, you will find something here.

It's been a privilege to witness the birth of this collection. I hope, as you read, you feel not only the depth of Lynne's voice, but also the echo of your own.

May these poems meet you where you are and walk with you along Paths Not Paved, to wherever you're going. Mostly, I want you to experience this collection in your own way and know that you are the "I" in this stanza from "Where was I":

> when I couldn't, didn't
> > do all I wanted or thought about
> > or jump with joy or invite you into me
> > or find all that there is or can be
>
> where I am now content.

Be content while reading this collection.

~ Julie Cummings, President, Columbine Poets, Inc.,
and author of *Ride of My Life*

INTRODUCTION

I'm proud to present my debut collection of poetry, written and rewritten over months and years in exploring existence through real and imagined thoughts, feelings, situations, people, and places. Piecing together words and images that describe an instant, hours, or long days is the challenge I enjoy in puzzling through the chasms of human experience.

In organizing the various poems into sections, I chose four themes. The first, *Yearning for More*, includes subthemes of solitude and connections, of companions and strangers, and of the passage of time. The second section, *Fleeting Mortality*, includes subthemes of loss and mortality as well as time and aging. In the third section, *Trusting Truths*, I've gathered my writings that speak to places and identities, to nature and beauty, and to family and self-discovery. The final chapter, *Paths Not Paved*, is also the title of the collection and includes reflections on urban alienation, connections to earth and the body, and simplicity.

In sharing my thoughts through poetry, I have tried to form images of how life quickly shifts, moves toward unknowns, and constantly challenges what seem to be firm beliefs. Humility and acceptance tend to guide me these days where I see my rigidity while trying to flow, where I can't change the past, and where I can only live the moment of now, fleeting quickly.

While you read a poem herein, I hope that you might see something new, look at life slightly differently, understand others a little more, and perhaps find a path not paved to explore.

~ Lynne

Butterfly Cloud

To Winter
A Villanelle

To winter now with time to go
to mountains, valleys, anywhere
and feel the cold, the wind, the snow

we stand in awe as angels flow
like children lay in snow aware
to winter now with time to go.

To warm our hearts to be aglow
but see above that trees are bare
and feel the cold, the wind, the snow

to show our love and then to know
we run away and then don't care
to winter now with time to go.

I want to be as one and grow
in open sun to share and bare
and feel the cold, the wind, the snow.

Let's hold this time to bend the bow
to arc above in love so rare
to winter now with time to go
and feel the cold, the wind, the snow.

Questing

Lover after lover, one and another—
differences lure them into tangoes
with perfection wanting in all.

Ambitions of romance spin in the hustle—
each lover strutting to seduce the other,
both smothered in hues of happiness pursued.

Smiles in their eyes shine hopes—
This is it! This is the one!
but all are lies of never-there love.

Still, suitors seek ideals of truelove
in each touch, all short-lived lust,
while expecting more yet accepting less.

Their dance continues from one to another,
from either-or to more, as they parade their goods
to find the right consumer sooner to allure.

Wooers wonder who they want, who they are
with her or him, damning their own doubts—
are they a shuffle of flings, all insensible swings?

Nothing changes their wanton longing
in every step of self-deception, a waltz of illusions
to find a conclusion—the quest continues.

But the music has slowed to a simple slide
not even in stride with their body or mind—
an unfamiliar rhythm for both to find.

May I have this dance?

Not Quiet

It's not quiet
playing instruments of life—
moving, shuffling, dancing

wildly present within nature around
animals, birds—their sounds surround
in performing a rousing raucous.

Hear the wind rubbing windows and doors,
soul lovers passionately roaring,
surprise barking, music lusciously loud.

Nothing is quiet.

Quiet is sleep, death, wilderness,
chilling aloneness, reaching depression—
deep, stopping the thinking.

Quiet is beyond this being who cannot
not think, not do, not be involved,
not be alive, but still reaches out

treasuring calm gifts of serenity
seeking bliss within
this brazen maze.

My Muse

where are you   my muse

now separate   we walk

but together   as you promised

we are complete   in bliss

                      can you   my muse

                      inspire   desires

                      fire   this being

                      this life   without being

                      apart   too long away

come   to be found

be new   to renew

us, me, you   now

Untethered

love
bursting through
untethered

passions
without boundaries
holding back, unlimited

yearning
no stopping
excitement, reviving unknown

senses
no words
to grasp, unfettered

awe
fleeting in time
intertwined

On the Express Train

On the city express train
not choosing to get off—
be somewhere new, a local place

a chance to seek calm
differences of maybes, perhaps
adventures, out-of-the-way choices

doorways, not better or worse
but potent possibilities of courage
to leave this path

to explore, replenish this self
the other within, who lacks time, energy—
easy reasons to fear

newness, other destinations.

Companions

End of day returning home to mechanical moans,
peopleless parts shouting at this resident

who seeks companions, not a whirring icemaker,
refrigerator, purring air conditioner, wine cooler

all performing orders like clocks
ticking, all chiming in rhyme in time.

No cell phone dings,
no one called, no one cares.

Steady instead, the automated mates
continue constant daily chores

as this dweller stands slumped, surrounded
by mocking mimics, phony fixes to ease this soul

yearning for something while encircled
in wealth meant to console.

Vintage vinyls, books beckon
from the cluttered coffee table.

The ready couch stares at the blank TV,
liquor bottles stand attent on the sidebar.

All wait to be engaged to excite the silence—
which one or two will fill these gaping gaps?

Lights switched on, brightening spaces
among pseudo suitors hugging hushed places.

TV turned on, background noises, comforting
voices console the soul, blind the mind.

Manufactured helpmates as devotees
distract from deafening defeat

with digital sounds like wraparounds—
an unending merry-go-round.

Rain taps gently on the roof.

Eyes Yes

I call her name, tell-all tail wagging
she comes to my feet, sits, looks
at me, eyes fixed on eyes

knowing, or I think she knows
but what does she know
I don't know

yet those eyes

like those of my lover speak love
in yeses in his eye-edges
wrinkles curving up in crescent moons
proving my hopes, I hope.

No creases outside the circles
of my dog's eyes, cocoa brown staring
steadily fixed to catch any slight yes-lets-play
body twitch from me—any will do.

My varied voice loud, soft to high
to low, quick to long, each tone
alerts her as ticking microseconds
telling her how I feel

just like his words seem to sing
to me, savoring each caressing note

as his eyes shout *Yes* like insights
inside, into his soul, heart, feelings
revealed as I gaze into his eyes
up close, or I just think it's so

it's what I want
in those eyes
in that *Yes*.

If Only

If only words would trickle quickly
down mind streams to flow eagerly
down peaks through foothills

icy in winter, sweet in summer
speckled with red yellows in autumn
regenerating to everywhere green in spring

inspiring anything, something to be
written as courage to speak silently, loud
on paper, digital pages, mud, sandstone

without dread of reality dripping, flooding
from this humanness bound in boulders
fixed on mountainside bosoms

hugging wide gullies, precipices too high
to challenge the climb while slipping in slippers
meant for standing still, moving flat

pleading to be outrageously surprised
to soar in new boots meant to cling
to hold steady as gravity pulls backwards

choosing, or not, to see
skies above, clouded, darkened
yet sunny blue in openings

urging spirits to sprint high
succumb to fascinating black holes
non-existent except as we create.

Now Here

Now here we are in love and see our truth
in hope, in trust to find the all of life
a goal to find how love can find our youth
not lost but sure to bring us close to strife.

We seek, don't find
the heaven inside
while wondering why
we wander by.

How can we see what we don't see right now
forever here so blind we come to hear
the words, the thoughts, the push, the pull, we feel.
Now here we are in love and see our truth.

Seeking Joy

From just ok to more, to find the awe
the awesome, the wholesome, the more
to find the passion, constant in each minute

in ecstasy, in joy—not possible

like weather morphs, like tides subside
the up and down, again, again
from left to right to middle

in ceaseless change

we are the seasons shifting, the fresh to foul
from births to deaths, all surging, cresting
then falling again, from stillness to fullness

or the other way round

night to day, my dark to your light, bridging
one to the other over rushing waters, waning
in winter, flowing slowly but still streaming

a current of wavering brilliance.

Breathing in the Breeze

Rhythms of the mind
in souls with one breath
their senses and beings
each wrapped around each

like the ocean gently lapping
far shores of long enduring
bringing music in concert
to the madness of living

for two who lay gazing
at placid clouds clinging
tumbling slowly with the flow
gently touching their essence

reaching magic in the moment
resting briefly on the sands
warmed well by a brightness
of light unseen before

laughing, lingering
longing for more
stillness seeking
passions fleeting

listening to the wind
to the beat, to the sound
of the waves in the heavens
breathing in the breeze.

Evening Sun in Early Fall

One by One

Death accumulates one by one.

Mother, father, family, friend
old, young, their lives unsung

no more to tell, their stories done—
if only we'd asked before they passed

their dances, chances flung to the wind
her life once there, his years once then.

One by one death lets us know,
one by one we see them go.

Death's intimate delusions
shout final conclusions.

All is gone for those who've ceased
who wanted to last or wanted to pass

all dear to us awakened to see
how now is to love, to live, to be

present in the present
as each moment lasts a moment.

Death by Train
    Tokyo, Japan

Within an inch
is death, a cinch—
a sure way
to part ways.

In front of the train
he leaps in shame
of loss or blame
on loves or pain.

Timing is crucial
for his final removal
that needs a plan—which track,
when to jump—all is black.

We don't shed a tear, don't care
about his hatred unabated, his despair—
we don't want to be depressed
over one life less, a mess full of stress.

Waiting for a train likely full already
we passively stand steady, ready

to board, all other ignored.

Strangers

I've seen you before, standing there
inviting me, though you don't know it
pulling me, a lure, to you assured.

I've seen you before, passing
in the parade as one of many
on a street, in a line, around a room.

I've seen you in a bar, on a bus
somewhere, your eyes, the look—
what is it?

I don't remember what you said
but your voice, soothing sounds
drenched me like a foggy flood.

I do remember how you made me feel
with few words—I'll stumble there
for even one night of mad love mania.

Or is it just madness, was it at all,
then, whenever, or was it just a shuffle
of deadbeats, derelict dates

strangers tossing their wares
toward me unaware.

Sakura Life

Sakura blossoms, pink and white
you grace your cherry trees

shading our way, urging us
to look up to hope, a sapphire sky.

Whispers of breezes coax you
to dance, to float and fill the air.

Ohanami! as the Japanese say
"gazing at flowers," treasuring beauty.

Your beloved blooms cascade over all
on picnickers, grave cleaners, walkers too.

Your gentle rain of countless blossoms
wraps us in a missive of beginnings.

You shower days in blissfulness
baptizing with life, a newness.

Spring is here.

Bald Eagle Bold

Ready to fly, bald eagle bold
broad wings unfold
to begin gliding toward
blue skies last soared.

Your egg-yolk beak points right
your rhombus frame shifts slight
your snowy head leads flight
toward cloud clusters white.

As king of this realm
leader at the helm
you find a dead tree
a throne where you see

all around all hushed—
your talons have crushed
small beings below
whose dashings were slow.

Like an avalanche beast
you swoop down for a feast—
a fast rabbit darts angles
and flees your death mangles.

Smart the rabbit's art!

My Day

Morning. I'm up with you when you awake.
Our routine begins. You ask *Outside?* I know
what it means because you open the door,
I go out, do my thing, return, wait for you
to open the door, then you take off my pajamas—
a sweater you put on me every night, I don't know why.

Now. I love to keep you company, sit on your lap
but I love soccer more—I wait for your feet
or his, hers, anyone's anywhere on any floor.
Ready steady alternating with my two front paws
I paddle my 5-inch orange ball directly between your feet
while I carry my pink rubber bone in my mouth
and it's a goal! Then you kick it back to me
in our living room soccer field, and I always win
when you kick it anywhere for me to go get it.

All day. I wait for soccer time because that's when
I know you love me enough to play with me.
Then later you feed me prescription food
and I know you love me because you pay
more, you told me, and I definitely understand
everything you say to me.

Occasionally. I know I'm an old lady so
I love the spa—*Thank you!*—the warm bath
hair trim, nail clipping, brushing that you arrange
with the groomer who is gentle because you explained—
Thank you!—and she listened to how I hate for anyone
to touch anything below my knees—*Thank you!*

Sometimes. I nibble-bite you if you surprise me
by brushing my paws too quickly or cleaning
my whiskered jaws decorated with dinner
and I've told you before and you do listen
so *Thank you!* for that and everything else
and I'll just go get a lapped-up sip of water now.

Continuous

From the side
an endless smile
on his elderly face.

On this city train
a continuous smile
is uncommon.

Illusion to conclusion—
This man's made it!
He's retired, had a good life.

Then he turned his head—
a stroke had forever fixed
his upside-down frown

leaving him unwillingly
in an unending presence
of supposed happiness

offering an indelible finale
of delusions in assumptions
of others—deceiving ourselves.

High Flight

The 8-inch white, plastic angel
had a second wing, now broken, tossed
lost somewhere.

Hanging noble on the restaurant wall
she heralds higher thoughts, not caring
about losses.

Centered alone, the sentinel dwells above
the day to day, dark through light, people
drinking, dining.

Clinging to fewer ambitions of divine flight
abiding closer to earthly beings, she serves
as guardian.

Treasured, she remains regal
constantly listening, watching
above all.

Enduring, endearing
the cherub smiles over all
hungry patrons.

If only to float freely like her, fully accepted
as she is, fractured yet poised, peaceful
in gazing

imagining immortal impossibilities.

Bingo Queen and King

Too many years ago, on Tuesdays near noon in the great bingo hall, the regular wishful gathered, addicted and delighted like a church family. Some chose to sit in the smaller room that used to be for non-smokers when smoking was still allowed in public. Closed off to the large hall, the smaller room had glass half-walls to see the rest of the congregation, and sound was piped in via wall speakers to hear the priestly edicts.

Praying always to win, the mostly elderly gamers got the "Early Bird" special, all eager to start the games at 12:15. These devotees bought for $1 each at least one, long paper sheet consisting of three bingo cards. Each separate card had five columns across labeled B, I, N, G, O and five rows below of random numbers with a "FREE" square in the middle. At the front of the crowded hall, the caller called out, *Any Way Bingo is a $25 win.* The games began.

A constant customer, my Bingo Queen mom came early to claim her front row seat in the smaller, used-to-be non-smoking room. She used to smoke, but now she just wanted the quiet of the smaller room. She would get ready, daubing her pink ink marker on the FREE middle spot on each of the recyclable paper bingo cards printed in Mexico. She bought 4 sheets of 3 games each, a total of 12 cards to check for the bingo numbers called. Mom still had quick eyes in her 70s, proving she could have been an accountant in the 1930s when she wanted to, but didn't get that scholarship to go to college.

My Bingo King dad was the announcer on the altar-like stage that Tuesday and began pulling out one of the bouncing balls from the clear box, bingo machine. Using a microphone, he read the ball, saying slowly, *Under "I."* Then waiting while feeding the excitement of the bingo players, he paused a few seconds, deliberately preparing the crowd for the next verbal gift of the number on the ball, he said, *25—That's I 25.* He continued to pull popping balls and announce each letter slowly, then its number, giving godly hopes to the churchly participants.

Next to me, I heard *BINGO!* The Bingo Queen proudly smiled, waving her floppy sheet high with the one winning card. The Checker walked over to her, called out the bingoed numbers on the card, and the royal announcer of the meeting sang, *That's a winner!* Disappointed bingoists asked table partners, *Were you close? How about you?* while a few damned their gods, sighing.

My Bingo King dad also called weekly mid-day bingo games at the local Veterans of Foreign Wars, his VFW Post where he was a member. Stationed at the Naval Air Station in Wildwood, New Jersey, in World War II, he flew as a gunner in the back of an SBD Dauntless, a Scout Bomber Douglas, over the seas nearby, checking for German subs along the US east coast, though never overseas in the so-called "foreign war."

Dad accompanied my Bingo Queen mom going every week to the bingo games at the VFW and the Bingo Palace, same days, times, rooms, people. Mom loved to play the game, always ready to go anywhere anytime. So, dad did too, as the caller.

That Tuesday, when I accompanied my mom just to be with her, the Bingo Queen smiled while praising her Bingo King who had just given her the win, *He's my man!*

White Orchid

Her Song
> *For our mothers*

Glorious as the song of a winter bird
fills bare trees with melodies
lovingly, lively
she soothed family and friends.

Splendid as spring flowers
open to the welcoming sun
gracious, giving
she blossomed each day.

Gentle as the summer mountain creek
glistens over ancient rocks
steady, stable
she smiled, radiating the hours.

Softly as the autumn leaves
glide quietly to the forest floor
tranquil, trusting
she finished her joy-filling journey.

Ode to 2 Wheels

We need your help to save our bones
to save our air, to save our homes.

We've paved your paths
for ease to please.

We've added racks for you to stand,
to lock you safe from thieving hands.

To stop your rusting
we do all adjusting.

We'll give you some oil,
some paint when you're old.

We'll keep the basket, keep the ringer,
change the light, add a blinker.

To avoid the end, we tend
and mend our proven friend.

Gone

Where have you been?

I miss the bliss you brought
too long ago to that shadow of me
longing, in search of infinity
open to unknown, grasping for new

everywhere, seeking strength
a liberating bolt, a whirlwind jolt
to shake my vanishing core, vibrate
this pleading soul into unstoppable fire

flames rising, forever lasting
moving me to roar, to scream
emotions into each empty edge
renewed, with a bottomless profound

passion

you've come at last from afar, a jumpstart
to my spirit unfurling like a fresh blossom
full of deep colors in perfumed essence as I quiver
in sweet western breezes warmed by your sun

shining upon this summer flower soaring
into fall, flowing to whispers waving,
hailing *Hello* to our senses as beams of life
light the dark, then, you're gone

winter is here.

The Old Bear
> *At the antique store*

High on the store shelf
the old stuffed bear stands
four paws firm
on four worn wheels
all in all two feet tall

tan fur faded by time
and times aboard his broad back
golden shoulder threads thinned
where young legs urged
each forward campaign.

The critter had many names
commands he obeyed
to please the eager rider
on quests and pursuits—
crusades of great worth

travels of fearless toddlers
along kitchen and parlor paths
living room mazes, hallway chasms
toward bedroom kingdoms—
trips in well-trodden territories.

Child voices, eager to conquer
charged *Faster, Faster*
as the child General
in early training was ruler
of the well-trained brute.

Today for purchase in old-age glory
the placid creature reigns
unattended, uncommanded
far above now older children—
grownups gazing up

living their vivacity past
on rocking horses, sticks, brooms
maybe never on a rolling bear
giving them now a brief chance
to ride their own steed of youth

in the present of the past.

Near Night

Winter's here, tilting spirits
into stillness, a tranquil evening

wrapped in whispers chilled
to awaken humble respect.

Our shared sun slips lower
tossing rays like pristine pathways

invitations to exploration in the hush
of days and nights to come.

Let's imbibe in lush cloud gestures
designing solar pinks then reds

as daylight dwindles behind mountain crests
before geese gather in safe lake havens

before clocks chime time
for the quiet of near night.

Clouds Over Pikes Peak

Side Dishes
>*Tucson, circa 1998*

Wandering down the street
wanting something to eat
glancing through windows
into restaurant shadows
I check out each place
but debate and hesitate.

I walk a bit more
then go through the door
of O'Malley's Bar & Grill
sit at the bar, wondering still
about a hamburger and fries,
seeing few suits or ties

just beers and cigarettes
baseball caps, cowboy hats
blonde blondes, all flirts
tight jeans, tight shirts
showing breasts or chests
muscles flexed to impress

hairdos sprayed, dyed to hide
hopes to get laid, all fears aside—
no one faces made-up faces,
everyone aims for other places,
smiles and styles that tease toward beds
setting the tone for the night ahead.

I see the play
don't want to stay
so I walk away
and find the Aroma Café—
selections, sides on display
all handmade, all gourmet.

The chef-clerk combo with a neat goatee
blue-painted thumbnails, beams at me
*A panini and what for a side, ratatouille,
garbanzos, feta, penne, or greens?
Mixed and tossed? Just here to please.*
Standup-ordering, this serves my needs!

Throughout the room, ballads then Mozart
the next guest raving about Jesus in his heart,
peace and how this music has no message
but his vision last night showed him a sage
a man with long locks who showed him the way
Thank God! showed him the way.

I take my tray to the tables outside
where a straggly, bearded, long-haired guy
shoots angry glares at ghosts he dreads,
shuffles while smiling to sounds in his head,
where lesbians ready each other to bed
nerds wishing they could, talking physics instead.

Cars passing. Walkers chatting.
Sun's out. I have no doubts.
The perfect plate, not ornate.
This fits my style. I'll stay awhile.

Cologne of pheromones.
I love the smell of musk.

Peninsular

In anonymity we wander
over beach and stone
unknown
passages intimate
horizons infinite.

Wave after wave
in synchronous chorus
opus continuous
upon shores anew
souls renew.

Traveling to Topeka

Oh, yes! Do slow down driving east through Kansas on interstate
I-70, the main mid-US artery. Can't miss this vista! Fences of
locally quarried, cream-colored stone columns, more or less
6 inches wide and 6 foot tall, linked by barbed wire to keep
cattle in, big critters out.

Our mid-country plains long ago were no longer an Open Range.
Few trees on this range to form into fences. Purposefully set by
earlier settlers over 150 years ago, the pastel pillars posed as
strength, doubled up at times by those who were doubting others
along long distances with few homesteads.

These faithful links of limestone marked meager human attempts
of separation to show possession of one's cattle and land claims.
Some markers fallen, others propped up by two similar posts, point
out our feeble failures at fixed fiefdoms. Enough standing stalwarts
stay, reminding us of past passions trying to protect possessions,
now gone.

Nature innately takes over these mostly treeless Midwest
flatlands, proudly displaying yellow-grey prairie grass, wildflowers,
antelopes, plain wildness. Still, a farmer's distant presence is known
today in sprawling vast fields, speckled with 5-foot-high rolled
wheels of hay waiting to be gathered, stacked.

On this fast-paced freeway, peaceful glancing is perturbed briefly
by speeding semi-trucks piggy-backed 2 to 3. Roaring modernity
erupts for a moment. The hotel in Topeka awaits. A swim, sauna,
scotch, room service, organic roast chicken salad.

Tranquility here, there, abundant in this Midland.

Where was I

when I fell off the end of a pier
    and my father dived deep into the lake
    to rescue me, a 2-year-old who wandered
    during a picnic in a park somewhere

when my first was born
    a wonderful marvel to me still young
    though older than my fellow mother friends
    and I felt like an all-knowing adult

when the world changed
    becoming complex, dangerous
    because we can see, hear more
    find it on the internet, watch TV, know more

when I became more
    than what I was
    because we met, grew
    together, apart, repeat

when you loved someone
    else, who I didn't know or did
    and I wanted to run, hide, leave, scream
    out, *Out of my life*, you, her, everyone

when life continued
    with and without me, alone
    while I contemplated how
    to make my mark on the world

when I couldn't, didn't
    do all I wanted or thought about
    or jump with joy or invite you into me
    or find all that there is or can be

where I am now content.

Boats of Burden

Bulging grey barges
four stories tall
linked one, two, to three
slide sluggishly along
the murky Chao Phraya River.

Dusty black raincoatings
cover unknown cargo
within these mammoth movers
slipping quietly up the river
rippling silvery in the sun.

On the first floating phantom
a durian-colored shack
eyeing the lentil-green water path
commands the elephantine triad
with their sleepy heads bowed.

Waving to the boat rhythm
two shirts dry, hanging upside down
outside the hut's door
showing someone serves
as master of these Siam slaves.

Who's atop, what's inside,
where's the weary way
taking these Bangkok beasts?

Treasured

Beloved butterfly, adorned in black and gold
you flitter shadows on the sunset canvas

shaping skies above purple mountains
framing rural landscapes with fields full

near sandstone canyons carved by rivers
deep blue-green, flowing to regal oceans

where a graceful whale glides quietly
under a billionaire's polished yacht

crafted from trees treasured more
by lions, birds, bees, me

and you.

The Waitress

In a modest cafe on the plaza in Santa Fe, she serves up what you're looking for—a menu of mainstays. With order pad in hand and constant smiles and laughs, she asks customers where they are from, then joyfully moves from one table to another, finally to mine. I turned the tables slightly and asked her about her. She came from New Jersey 30 years ago because she hated crowds, congestion, distance from nature. Holding on to her Jersey accent, she says she's wild. Offers to split the bread pudding with me if I don't want a whole one.

Six Native Americans, who sell their wares in the porticos across the plaza, come in for lunch, all well known to this waitress. They each cheek-kiss her, and her them, while she holds their hands as she greets each one, saying each person's name while she gazes long into their eyes. One native woman whispers in her ear, and the full-of-glee server beams in a pause of calm caring.

Caressing a wad of dollar bills 3-inches thick, she makes change for patrons paying their bill. She doesn't realize how she has changed them as weary-warn guests, now fed well, warmed into easy smiles. With false teeth, she slides her mouth sidewise when she speaks. In her presence, no one notes such minutia or her plumpness when they're being cared for heartfully.

Worthy of an Emmy. A daily unrehearsed performance of kindness, joviality. A star-studded show for locals, for travelers stopping for personal nourishment that she gives freely, unknowingly. She's the draw, the advertisement, the luck of the town, the pull of the plaza. I bow to you in thanks and praise you—the best of us in being who you are, serving up the best of our life menu.

Homecoming

Wash, scrub, wax, rub
clothes, doors, walls, floors.

Rugs ragged! Cut the strings.
Oh my, such little things!

Dust drips hanging—sweep the ceilings.
I try to calm these nervous feelings.

Sew the splits in couch and chairs.
Wash the dogs, brush their hair.

Right clothes? I look too fat!
Lipstick on. Hair's too flat!

Didn't do this! What about that?
Never mind! I don't have time!

She's coming home!
She's coming home!

She's vegan, so no meat, no fish.
Will she like this tofu dish?

Lentils stewed, broccoli steamed,
potatoes baked to suit her taste.

Now at ease. Table's set, all to please.
Napkins, placemats, all to match.

In center place, a flower vase
blue-green glazed, in perfect space

her high school project she chose to reject
I treasured always and quietly kept.

In it I place curved slender stems
covered in blooms, small yellow gems

with red-dot middles all gathering *Yes!*
a bowing, welcoming, resounding *Yes!*

Motor. Taxi. Shuffle. Door.
Hugs. Kisses. Tears and more.

You're home! You're home!
We've waited so long. All sadness gone.

You light this life—your name means heart.
All days in all you see the art.

The flowers look pretty, Mom!

December Morning Moon
in the West

Lightning Bugs

Small town America! You know your own—you take care
to be the mystical, fairytale town that hides from cityness,
hides from life that might appear at your doorstep someday
when you become afraid, bolt your doors, lock all windows.

Your folk are trusting, friendly, welcoming
as your nightly fireflies fling me back to my childhood
at 3 years old, years ago catching magical flies in jars
on your dark lawns oozing the steam of the day from earthen pores.

I would stand amazed at light from invisible, harmless insects
I wanted to capture, to see them, to understand
what they are, how they do what they do
but catching them was a challenge.

I'd jump at a light that I missed because it had moved
as I looked for the lightning in a moment
as I seem to do each day, now older
not able to hold moments in a jar—they might die

like my dreams if I don't let them go
let them be, rather than chase them endlessly
leaping in expectation and disappointed
at not catching the light, the moment.

Your town sleepily gives me lightning bugs, unlocked doors
open windows, friendly folks, fresh mowed lawns, families
walking down the street after dinner, dogs running free nearby,
teenagers not burdened with curfews.

Small town America! You're free,
still there, lightening life.

Moon Moment

Her mass looms large,
brighter at early morning 6am

30 earths away, unimaginable
yet close in the universe expanse.

Stilled, a sense of insignificance—
minuteness in her immenseness

I feel frailty within vastness
rattling this essence

surprised, gently jarred by her—
an impact enduring.

In this moon moment, immersed
treasuring time

sharing enormity in smallness
I measure mine.

Love Isn't

Love isn't always what you think
what you wanted, what you hoped
but fits instead among unknowns
as all depends on thoughts uncloaked.

Love isn't drawn or written down
but rather changing as evoked
to be what is, the now, unseen
unplanned, just present, not invoked.

I'm Always Here
A Rondeau

I'm always here for you, for now
in all the ways my mind knows how
in every way you've done for me
for all the years as you would see
how life has given smiles and frowns.

We've given all we can, for now
to ours and theirs as families shall
do all we can to love and please.
I'm always here.

You're always there as with a vow
in words, in actions—you know how
in fields of life not planned to be
and did the best we could, you see
let's celebrate and take a bow.
I'm always here.

Paths Not Paved

Rockies on a February Morning

Inside Insides

Walls, windows open or closed—
frames that form lives within.

Rigid rooms doing their best
define, divide duties and deeds.

Hallways all ways connecting the rest—
my schisms, your rhythms orchestrate space.

Floors, mosaics support the weight
of hours and days we hesitate.

Cabinets, cupboards hold histories high—
our treasured trappings, precious pieces.

Closets hide hapless hangings
for naked fears to cover flaws.

Tables for talking, dining, crying.
Chairs for pausing, discussing, fussing.

Hopes and dreams at desk, in bed—
one place to write, one to put right.

Puzzles to juggle, troubles to shuffle
words to blend, minds to mend.

Inside insides, nothing put aside—
all bodes well in this abiding abode.

The Rush

Forgive me

for your feet stepped on, bags bumped
shoulders knocked, coats flapped,
bodies pushed, arms shoved, hands hit

eyes not contacted, smiles not returned
seats not given up, words not said.

I am selfish in the rush
to get where I'm there.

I scream inside, others despised
who do the same. No one to blame

in this hustle of hurry—
humanity insanity

except to accept
slower, calmer.

Sounding

    music, sounds felt, melt
            into the whole, the soul
    vibrating, shaking
            cells, the essence
    of heartbeats pulsing

    veins like violin strings
            played, stroked
    by a magic wand
            the bow of fine hairs
    sliding over this being

    gliding through notes
            held long, softly touched
    tuned tones lifting
            the core toward other
    living ways to be the beat

    above the base, above all else.

Numbered No Ones
Post Office Coda, Colorado Springs

68? 67? 66?
5? 4? 3? 2?

she sing-sang loudly
slowly lilting upward the ending
of each number for all to hear clearly.

I guess there just AIN'T
nobody out there

she sing-sang loudly
from behind her counter.

A very large, strikingly beautiful
postal worker with blond streaks
through her long, wavy brown hair

looked around, again, around
ready to help anyone with one
of those numbers who wanted service.

I guess they're there,
but they just ain't ready

she sing-sang loudly
smiling while sharing
her sing-song happiness.

Ok, next?

Loved it—standing, waiting
in that long line, first time ever
entertained by a clerk in a Post Office.

Medicine Wheel

Part of us, our medicine, our wheel, integrated into our wholeness, being part of nature, the earth, together, in ourselves, in nature, here, now, one.

North—
White, wisdom, winter, the buffalo giving its entirety to Native Americans for their survival. Now for us giving ourselves to our own nature to those around, in a centered way, seeing the wheel, walking through and with life as a whole, on solid ground, a time to integrate the past. Fine seed pods, white curly leaves, growth, fineness, clarity, softness, naturalness, willingness—to be blown with the winds, coming from one growth and beginning another.

East—
The golden eagle flying over, getting a larger perspective, freedom, yellow, the rising sun, birth, creation, newness, beginnings of growth, spring, letting go of the rush, seeking peace in life of the moment, letting it happen more easily, saying it just doesn't matter, letting go of perfection-seeking.

South—
The mouse, seeing things close up in detail, red, summer in the full living cycle, active and dynamic growth, fiery excitation about a growing and vibrant existence.

West—
The bear, black, autumn, retrospection, recognizing death is part
of this cycle, getting ready for another birth and rebirth, a time
to look at the past growth cycle, accept that all comes to an end
and that's ok.

Center—
Where we lay, all in a circle with bare feet touching, connecting
to the earth, sensing the wind, the cool, the sun, the shadows,
the colors passing in front of our eyes, solidly on the ground
supporting us, all creators, our own creating within abilities
to center ourselves through our own creating, recognizing all
of our cycles.

All directions—
Part of us, our medicine, our wheel, integrated into our wholeness,
being part of nature, the earth, together, in ourselves, in nature,
here, now, one.

Eclipse Seen on the Sidewalk

Deliverance

On the busy train platform
uniformed, white-gloved pushers
blow shrill whistles and gently press
commuters to jam even tighter
into already-packed trains.

The officials shout ritual words,
whistle again, warning the crowd
deafened by headphones,
doors are closing.

Well-dressed Tokyo customers obey
the early morning crawling, rushing
to deliver themselves to cram
into precisely timed trains railing
to Corporate Centrality, the reigning kingdom.

Those last in—stoic, stone faces
flattened, merging with train windows
as they stand, eyes glazed
staring at passing life outside.

Not able to move, poised as posts
strangers touch closely, never speaking—
otherwise disturbs crowded silence
posing intimate possibilities.

Slightly cologned, unwilling automatons
stare straight, not chancing to glance
at anyone shoved into close proximity
as few descend and more press in
at each new stop, same thing.

Stance

Crammed city train
stops as scheduled.

Push-nudged boarding
passengers stumble in safely
slightly touching, gently bumping
others barely budging.

I see you—taller than all, standing
firm, fixed like you're forever planted,
your hand gripping the hanging white loop
at arm's length steadying your stiff stance.

Defying the crowd's urge to move
you're unmoved, stubborn to stay
to keep your stand while others demand
your attention to shift, you won't.

I watch you stare, not blinking, burdened
by people's essence, presence, press-pushing
your buttocks, arms as they squeeze by
to find a place to be, to stare between others.

Today must be your *I don't care who you are*
or your day of *I'm pretending not to see you*
or maybe that well-known human mood
Don't you dare bother me.

I don't know you, don't want to,
don't care about the who of you,
the what made you this, the when
you became stone, the why.

But I could hope for your sake it's your moment
of *Sorry I didn't see you* or maybe an instance
of *I was thinking of something else* or possibly
your time for *I'm dozing awake I'm so tired.*

Whatever, wherever you are standing there
you're not here where others are in the tide
flowing in, out, with hopeful ease
to relieve the uneasy beat of bodies

tight in a quiet internal fight toward calm.

Centering

Angles, corners of this mind
stretching to sense the point
somewhere inside, outside

or is it seeing, hearing a focus, locus
someplace else—in the middle
top, bottom, core of this mortal

but where is this center merging
mindfulness, not thinking—has to be
feeling or is it being, this brain seeking

striving, struggling, chanting *Ohmmmm*
tossing around *Ho hum* and *Oh, hmmm*—
don't know, still trying

not supposed to try
or to do, but to calm, to be
just there—where?

Jungle Lane
Southeast Asia

Snake-curved earthen walking lane
flat with edges a brick high
hugging jungle on the other side—
humanity holds back nature
in this empty park in Asian urbanity

where I'm my guide after hefty meetings
nearby and I stroll this path, no control,
faltering in ridiculous high heels,
in these shoes trying to protect
what naked feet don't.

Wobbling-worried I cross a rapid stream
via a stone bridge tilting, my heeled feet teetering,
tipping in these leathered trappings,
hobbling, barely navigating this wild walkway
with waving wide cracks, artistic ripplings

along this winding walk next to undisturbed life
of nature's origins, edging this man-made track
within this precious land within the city hustle—
a trek to take, a haven for the dressed-up
away from livid formality to vivid reality

a refuge, a reset.

Body Beautiful

Flesh—how I welcome your pleasure
while wrestling with wrinkles,
timelines of wisdom and wit.

Hair—how I feel blonde-red
seeing platinum instead,
better than rubies, you said.

Hands—how I caress yours
gliding over this bountiful body
receiving riches in subtle strokes.

Skin—how I sense touch
from sun rays, your ways
caressing calmly, caring.

Voice—how I sing silent
in concert with your rhythms
rippling on corporal waves.

Eyes—how I see deeply
from the past to be present within,
with you here, beyond and there.

Mind—how I climb to clarity
clocking days tumbling terrifyingly
toward unknowns and your distance.

Body—how we've moved mountains
measured in spoonfuls spilling
slowly into now with you, wherever.

Camping

Smell the outdoors—
pine, air, nature,
campfire smoke.

Feel the sun's heat,
taste rain drops, touch all—
stones, tree needles, dirt.

Summers for time aside,
weekends by streams, lakes
in the woods, mountains, high plains.

Hear the love at the picnic table
full of family, friends sharing
campfire food, smiles, comfort.

In Mom and Dad's camper I read
my favorite book tossing lines
taking me time-traveling.

With lines tossed in their lake lanes
others are fishing and sit, wait
serene, mind-traveling somewhere.

With time to gaze at wilderness close by
I wander on my canvas, drawing, painting
lines, curves catching angles

heights, colors, shades of pines
Aspen branches, a distant log cabin
at a distance to find elsewhere

the point of it all.

The Child in Me

The child in me alive and free
takes over the age that I am, you see.

I joke and I laugh at all that I can
to lighten my day, strengthen my stand.
I play and I smile a lot, you may think
to avoid and dismiss any problems to fix.

I don't give a care how others compare
how they believe I act young and very naive,
how I haven't learned yet or refuse to accept
adultness so frigid, imposing and rigid.

I know of the troubles, the sadness and pain
that we humans so clearly are surely to blame.
I know of my sins, my weaknesses too.

But I don't want to dwell on worldly hell
to keep me from being the best that I can
in a happier, brighter, more positive stand
that creates all the beauty as well as the beasts
while I cling to the former instead of the least.

If I don't, I can't see what the future may be
of the possible life outside of the strife.
It's my nature it seems to build upon dreams.

It's natural, you see, for a person like me
to have mostly a smile that is all worthwhile,
not the other way round with a frown and so down.

I could certainly choose the ugly to be
but that doesn't help me or others to see
what we have is all present, quite real, quite pleasant.

All we need is to believe what it takes to achieve
and the patience to do what we dream to come true.

I don't and I won't seek the black and the bleak.
I've got to see more, explore all the lore.
I've got to seek bright, all the love and delight
in all on life's street, in all whom I meet
to find what I've sought, enjoy the whole lot.

If child-like means, I continue to dream,
if childish is my seeking my bliss,
if young and naive means love and believe
my fantasies, fairies, and tales of fine princes
that could happen to me, allow me to be free,
then childish, child-like, naive may I be.

Rocky Mountain Stream

Voyage

Your story is a tumbling stream
rumbling over unexpected crags
carrying rocky debris

falling through eons to the bottom

sands sifting, shifting to rise
in your well-worn hands
lifting petite pebbles in littoral waters

hugging comforting shores

with currents lingering
in a swirling eddy, then serene
you reenter the flow

you rise from depths

tidbits of smiles happen
while waltzing, limping with pain
in a never-ending dance

of falling then climbing

to steep plateaus through feared feats—
all aching forays into the worthwhile,
a territory with views at last

you win.

Sky Riding

Above arching hills to ocean waters
heaving, flying upward along Monterey Bay
through white-patched, silver morning mist

all in line, air floating, linear linked
a pelican foursome glides in flawless formation
traveling together in their northward migration.

One after the other copies the one ahead
imitating each other in exact rhythm
wings up, down in silent orchestration

following the leader of the quartet
waving in the air—a ribbon of heaven
not far behind another pelican stream of fifteen.

In search of savory sea specimens, the group of four
roller coaster over the wet market below
cruising low, skimming the wavering blue water

then rising cloudward, dipping down
trying again at the bay's edge to no avail—
nothing today as they move on their way.

Nearby a legion of faithful friends
of half-a-hundred birds, a squadron
of feathered dive bombers winding

sliding, sky sailing in an imperfect V flowing
up, down, not diving today, no one departs
the flotilla family focused on the migrant mission.

Perfect time to scoop a feast, if you please—
a peaceful day for Pacific coast sky riding
for all free to dive, to rise, to ride the airs

share the heavens, hold the clouds, go
north, return south in a year, repeat the feat
vast miles each day, forward

riding the skies.

Country Acres Iris

Where the Flowers Go

I wonder where the flowers go
here now, then brusquely, suddenly not
when western winds will wildly blow

not leaving beauty on stems to rot
but throwing forth a summer breeze
that's comforting in nature's plot

for colorful blossoms that fear a freeze
to ride upon the playful gusts before the snow
to dance with joy to drift with ease

as all would hope to find the flow
in living through each wish-filled day
to see prized petals float high and low

then quickly uplift far to stay
on waves of air that weave their way.

Morning Setting Moon

ACKNOWLEDGMENTS

A heartfelt gratitude to my husband Tom for his honest reviews and critiques of my draft poems, thrown to him wildly and typically without context.

An enduring thanks to the Columbine Poets of Colorado and to the National Federation of State Poetry Societies for giving me a welcoming community of engaging poets.

A sincere appreciation for the well-known poet artists who served as willing contributors to provide comments on this collection: Diane Glancy, Lynda La Rocca, and Valerie Szarek.

In particular, I am deeply grateful to Julie Cummings for her invaluable input, her never-ending positivism, and for writing the "Foreword."

Finally, I applaud my editor Joe Cavanaugh and graphic designer Mark Terry for their innovative publishing activities promoting poetry. I am sincerely thankful to them for accepting me into their family of authors.

White Mountain Shasta Daisy

LYNNE A. McNAMARA BIOGRAPHY

Lynne McNamara has lived a rich and full life. As a teacher and administrative director in the field of international education, she has wandered and lived in Europe, the Middle East, and Asia—all gifting her the music of lives lived differently than within her US home. Living and working in Italy, Egypt, and Japan gave her the opportunity and gift of understanding other cultures. In accepting other realities, she opened her belief systems to the wide world of diversity in humanity.

In her mid-life journaling, she saw the poetic elements in her writing and began expanding her word artistry. Besides teaching writing and poetry, she established poetry readings at Temple University Japan in Tokyo and at the University of Maryland University College (now the University of Maryland Global Campus). Recently she served as a judge of poetry for the Art in Public Places Program in Loveland, Colorado, and for the National Federation of State Poetry Societies.

Sunset Rays

As an emerging author in later life, she treasures her time to write and reflect. Lynne loves to be immersed with family, friends, nature, and sunsets as well as gourmet food, all of which contribute to her writing poetry that moves her toward other. For Lynne, poetry is word art, painting the multidimensional flows of life to share with others in their own quests for understanding.

She received her Bachelor's degree in Italian with a minor in Spanish and her Master's in Linguistics from the University of Colorado Boulder. She was the youngest faculty member at CU Boulder as an Instructor in the Department of Italian at the age of 22. In her late 40s, she pursued and completed a PhD in Educational Administration and Higher Education at Southern Illinois University Carbondale.

Her life has been a history of opening new doors and following paths not paved.

****

Poetic works recently published:

Columbine at 45: Keeping Poetry Alive! (2023): "Leafing"

Art in Public Places Program, Loveland CO (2023-2024), an ekphrastic poem: "Earth gift"

California Quarterly, Volume 50, Number 1 (2024): "Quick"

National Federation of State Poetry Societies (NFSPS).
Poets for Peace—Sunflowers Rising: Poems For Peace Anthology
(May 19, 2025): "Child of the World"

International Women's Writing Guild (IWWG).
Write Forward: A Constellation of Voices
(September 15, 2025): "Alone and Together"

Buster  Bodhi
PRESS

The author's best friend.

Mark Terry   Joe Cavanaugh

We are poets and writers publishing poets and writers, focused on both the smallest detail and the far horizon.

If you are looking for a publisher to share your passion for writing, one that understands that every word matters and quality drives success, we are here for you.

Contact:

Joe Cavanaugh
jcavanaugh1@gmail.com

Mark Terry
markajterry@gmail.com

Made in the USA
Coppell, TX
10 February 2026